First published January 2013 by
South West Yorkshire Partnership NHS Foundation Trust
Fieldhead
Ouchthorpe Lane
Wakefield
WF1 3SP

A catalogue record of this book is available from the British Library ISBN 978-1-907717-04-8

This book was written by Kerry Delaney.

Kerry is an occupational therapist who works for South West Yorkshire Partnership NHS Foundation Trust.

Occupational therapists help people do things for themselves.

The Trust works to help people live life to the full.

Lots of people helped with this book. A big thank you to everybody who helped.

Lots of people with a learning disability helped to:

- Choose recipes
- Test the recipes
- Taste the food

A special thank you to Neal Pudsey, Nicky Serlin, Francoise Murphy and Aydn Fitchett.

Other people who helped with the book:

Emily Lam is a Dietician and helped make the food healthier.
Janet Marsh is a Food Hygiene Trainer and looked at how to make the food safe. Louise Toth is a Communication Project Coordinator and helped make the book easy to read.

Contents

About this Book

The recipes in this cook book have been made easy, so you can do more on your own.

The recipes are easy because:

- they are step by step
- you only need to do one thing at a time
- it doesn't matter how long it takes
- there are photos and easy words
- everything is measured and timed, so you don't have to guess

Things you will need in the kitchen

At the start of every recipe there is a page that tells you what things you will need to make the meal.

You might need more help with the recipe if you don't have all the things you need.

There are some things that you might not have in your kitchen. You might need someone to help you to buy them.

Electric Cooker

Electric cookers are easy to use because the dials have numbers on them.

If you have a gas cooker, you might need somebody to help you:

- Change the cooking times in the book
- Change the temperatures in the book
- Put numbers on the dials of the hob

Measuring Cups and Measuring Spoons

Measuring Cups and Measuring Spoons are needed for nearly all of the recipes.

They are an easy way to know how much food to put in a meal.

You can buy measuring cups and measuring spoons at a big supermarket or in a kitchen shop.

Buy ones with big numbers written on the handle.

Digital Scales

Digital scales have big numbers on and are easy to read.

Some people need help to learn how to use them.

Digital Timer

A digital timer tells you how long to do something, like stirring or cooking food in the oven.

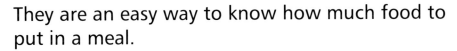

A digital timer is used in nearly every recipe in all of the books in this range.

Choose an easy digital timer with only 2 or 3 buttons.

A digital timer is better than a dial timer:

- It has buttons and a screen with numbers on it.
- The noise of a digital timer is easier to hear

In some recipes when the timer is set for a long time, you will see this picture:

You don't have to stay in the kitchen, but don't leave the house! Take the digital timer with you so you can still hear it make a noise.

How to use this book

This book can help you cook meals by yourself, or with a little bit of help.

This book can help you eat healthier food, look for this picture this means the dietician says it is healthy.

Help you might need

Everyone who helped make this book needed help to learn how to use some of the things in the kitchen. You might need some help to start with.

After people had learned to use the things in the kitchen, most people didn't need help to cook the meals, or only needed a little bit of help.

Some people need help to get the food and things from the kitchen they need, but can then cook the meal on their own.

Some people need help to buy the food and other things for the recipes, but can then cook the meal on their own.

Some people need help to put things in and out of the oven but can do everything else on their own.

Some people need help to open tins and packets but can do the rest on their own.

Some problems people have had

I get the measuring spoons and measuring cups mixed up
You could ask someone to mark with a permanent pen which are the cups and which are the spoons.

I don't understand what a "quarter" measuring cup or spoon is
Say the numbers as you see them - a 1/4 measuring cup, is easier if it is said "one four cup" rather than "a quarter cup".

This is the same for a 1/2 measuring cup – a "half" cup. Call it a "one two" cup.

Or you could put coloured dots or ribbons on the cups and spoons and put the same coloured dots in the cook book.

I don't know how to use a digital timer
Ask someone to help you every time until you don't need to ask for help any more.

I don't know how to turn my oven on
Ask someone to help you write on your oven, like in this photo.

My oven dial doesn't have all the temperatures written on it
Write the temperatures you need on the oven dial with a permanent pen or use stickers and write on the stickers.

You can write the missing numbers on your microwave too.

I don't know which dial turns on which hob ring.
Ask someone to help you with colours or numbers to help you know which one is which.

I can't use a tin opener
Tin openers are difficult to use. You could buy an electric tin opener. Ask for help to learn how to use it.

Tuna and Egg Salad

 Enough food for 2 meals

 This is a healthy meal
It can help you stay healthy

Food you need

1 Tin of tuna in spring water

30ml Olive oil

1 Packet of fresh parsley

15ml Red wine vinegar

2 Eggs

2 Pieces of spring onion

1 Tin of chickpeas

2 Tomatoes

1 Bag of lettuce

If you can't find something, ask the staff in the shop to help you

Things in the kitchen you need

Electric cooker

Eating spoon

Chopping knife

Big pan

15ml Measuring spoon

Chopping board

Big mixing bowl

Kettle

Tin opener

Plate

Digital timer

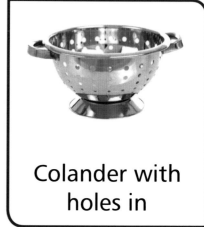
Colander with holes in

Wash and dry hands

Before you start cooking;

Get out all of the food you need.

Get out all of the things you need to cook with

Fill the kettle with water

Turn the kettle on

When the kettle has boiled

Pour water into the pan

Not to the top

Put the pan on the hob

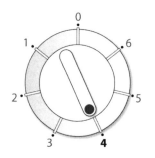

Turn hob to 4

0400

Set the digital timer for **4 minutes**

When the timer makes a noise

HOT

Get an eating spoon

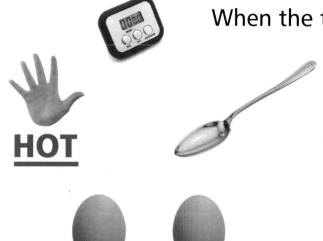

Put 2 eggs in the pan

  Set the digital timer for **8 minutes**

Come back when the timer makes a noise

When the timer makes a noise

 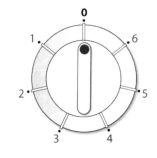 Turn **off** the hob

The eggs will be very hot

HOT

 Get the eggs out of the pan with a spoon

 Put the eggs on a plate

Open the tin of tuna

Squeeze the water out of the tin into the sink

Put all the tuna into a bowl

Wash and dry hands after touching tuna

Take the washing up bowl out of the sink

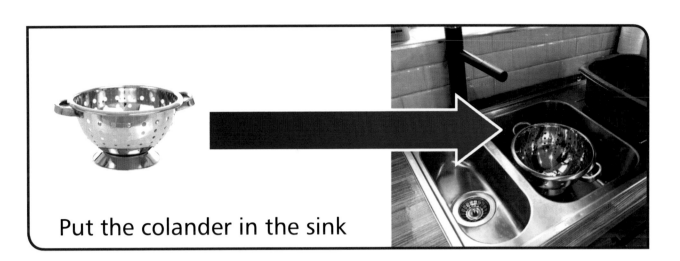

Put the colander in the sink

Open the tin of chickpeas

Put the chickpeas in the colander

Put all the chickpeas into the bowl

Put 2 pieces of spring onion on the chopping board

 Chop the spring onion

Put all the spring onion in the mixing bowl

 Wash and dry hands after touching the spring onion

 Get the **15ml** measuring spoon

  **1**

Put 1 spoon red wine vinegar in the bowl

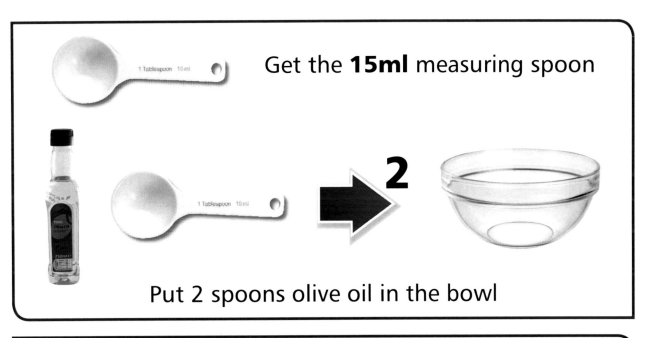

Get the **15ml** measuring spoon

2

Put 2 spoons olive oil in the bowl

6

Pick 6 sprigs of parsley

Wash the parsley under the tap

Put the parsley on the chopping board

Chop the parsley into small pieces

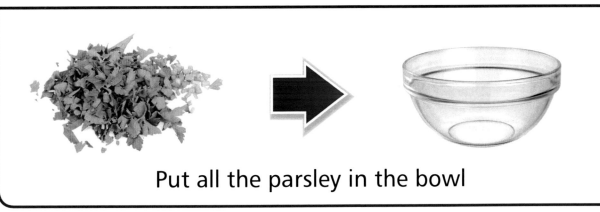

Put all the parsley in the bowl

Put a handful of lettuce in a mixing bowl

Set the digital timer for **2 minutes**

Stir everything in the bowl

Keep stirring until the timer makes a noise

When the timer makes a noise

Wash the tomatoes under the tap

Put tomatoes on the chopping board

Chop each tomato into 4 pieces

Put all the tomato in the bowl

Take all the shell off the eggs

   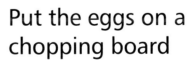

Put the eggs on a chopping board

Chop the eggs in half

Put all egg in the bowl

Ready to eat!

Wash up

Put everything away

Put any leftover salad in the fridge

Eat it tomorrow or put in bin

Chicken Stew

 Enough food for 2 meals

 This is a healthy meal
It can help you stay healthy

Food you need

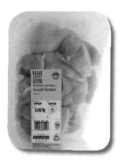

About 400g diced chicken

2 x 15ml Measuring spoon of gravy

1 Pack of casserole mix

If you can't find something, ask the staff in the shop to help you

Things in the kitchen you need

Digital timer

Electric cooker

Oven gloves

Oven dish with a lid

Plastic box with a lid

1 Pint measuring jug

Mixing spoon

Kettle

15ml Measuring spoon

Wash and dry hands

Before you start cooking;

Get out all of the food you need.

Get out all of the things you need to cook with

 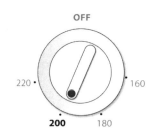

Turn oven on to 200

Put all the chicken in the oven dish

Wash hands after touching chicken

Put **all** the casserole vegetables in the oven dish

Fill the kettle to the top line with water

Turn it on

When the kettle has finished boiling

Pour water into the measuring jug

Fill it to the top

HOT

Pour all the water into the oven dish

 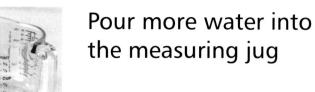

Pour more water into the measuring jug

Fill it to the top

HOT

Pour all the water into the oven dish

   **2**

Get a 15ml measuring spoon

Put 2 spoons of gravy into oven dish

 **02 00** Set the digital timer for **2 minutes**

 Stir everything in the oven dish

Keep stirring until the timer makes a noise

 When the timer makes a noise

Put the lid on the oven dish

Put oven gloves on   Put oven dish in the oven

  Set the digital timer for **60 minutes**

Come back when the timer makes a noise

When the timer makes a noise

 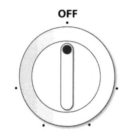

Turn **off** the oven

Take oven dish
out of the oven

Put on oven gloves

Ready to eat!

Wash up

Put everything away

When the stew is cold put it in a plastic box with a lid

Put it in the fridge

Eat it tomorrow or put in bin

Baked Spaghetti Bolognaise

 Enough food for 2 meals

 This is a healthy meal
It can help you stay healthy

Food you need

15ml Measuring spoon
of vegetable oil

2 Servings of spaghetti

1 Jar of bolognaise sauce

About 500g minced beef

1 Measuring cup
frozen mushrooms

1/2 Measuring cup of
grated cheese

If you can't find something, ask
the staff in the shop to help you

Things in the kitchen you need

Electric cooker

Oven dish

Oven gloves

1 Pan

Mixing spoon

Digital timer

15ml Measuring spoon

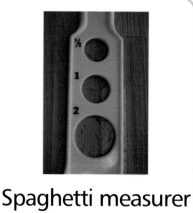

Spaghetti measurer

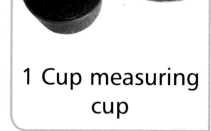

1 Cup measuring cup

1/2 Measuring cup

Plastic box with a lid

Wash and dry hands

Before you start cooking;

Get out all of the food you need.

Get out all of the things you need to cook with

 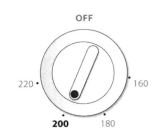

Turn oven on to 200

Get the **15ml** measuring spoon

Put 1 spoon of oil in pan

Put all the mince in the pan

Wash and dry hands after touching mince

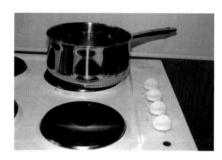 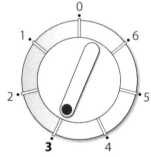

Put pan on the hob

Turn hob to 3

 **06 00**

Set the digital timer for **6 minutes**

Stir everything in the pan

Keep stirring until the timer makes a noise

When the timer makes a noise

Pour all the bolognaise sauce into the pan

Get a **1** cup measuring cup

Fill the measuring cup with frozen mushrooms

Put the mushrooms in the pan

 Get the **1** cup measuring cup

Fill the cup to the top with water

 Pour all the water into the pan

 **0500** Set the digital timer for **5 minutes**

 Stir everything in the pan

Keep stirring until the timer makes a noise

When the timer makes a noise

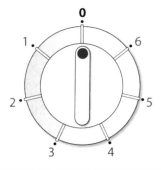

Turn **off** the hob

Measure 2 servings of spaghetti

Snap the spaghetti in half

Put spaghetti in oven dish

Put all the bolognaise mixture into the oven dish

Put oven gloves on

Put oven dish in the oven

 **IS00** Set the digital timer for **15 minutes**

Come back when the timer makes a noise

When the timer makes a noise

Put oven
gloves on

Take oven dish
out of the oven

 **02 00** Set the digital timer for
2 minutes

 Stir everything in the oven dish

 Keep stirring until the
timer makes a noise

When the timer makes a noise

Get the **1/2** measuring cup

Fill the measuring cup with grated cheese

Put the grated cheese into the oven dish

Put oven
gloves on

Put oven dish
in the oven

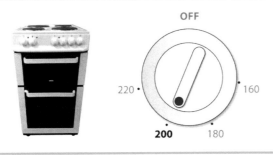 Check oven is still on 200

  Set the digital timer for **10 minutes**

Come back when the timer makes a noise

When the timer makes a noise

Put oven gloves on

Take oven dish out of the oven

 Ready to eat!

Wash up

Put everything away

When the spaghetti bolognaise is cold put it in a plastic box with a lid

Put it in the fridge

Eat it tomorrow or put in bin

Noodles with Ham and Peas

Enough food for 1 meal

The soy sauce in this meal has a lot of salt in
It is ok to eat as a treat now and again

Food you need

1 Carrot

15ml Measuring spoon vegetable oil

1/2 Measuring cup frozen peas

2x15ml Measuring spoon soy sauce

4 Slices ham

1 Pack straight to wok noodles

1/4 Measuring spoon minced garlic

2 x 15ml Measuring spoon sweet chilli sauce

If you can't find something, ask the staff in the shop to help you

Things in the kitchen you need

Electric cooker

Grater

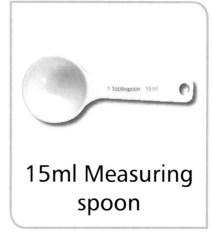

15ml Measuring spoon

Big pan

Mixing spoon

1/4 Measuring spoon

Mixing bowl

Chopping knife

Chopping board

Plate

Digital timer

1/2 Measuring cup

Wash and dry hands

Before you start cooking;

Get out all of the food you need.

Get out all of the things you need to cook with

 **1**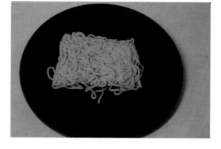

Open 1 packet
of noodles

Put the noodles
on a plate

Wash the carrot
under the tap

Put the carrot on the chopping board

Chop both ends off the carrot

Grate all the carrot

Put all the carrot in mixing bowl

Get 4 slices of ham

Put the ham on the chopping board

Chop the ham into pieces

Put all the ham in the mixing bowl

Wash and dry hands
after touching the ham

Get the **15ml** measuring spoon

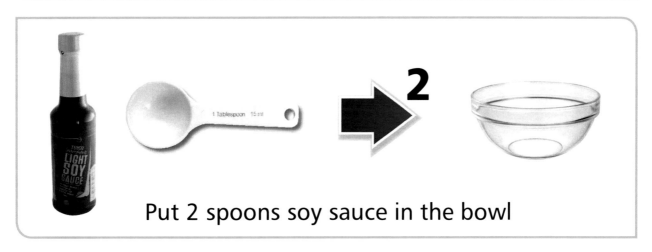

Put 2 spoons soy sauce in the bowl

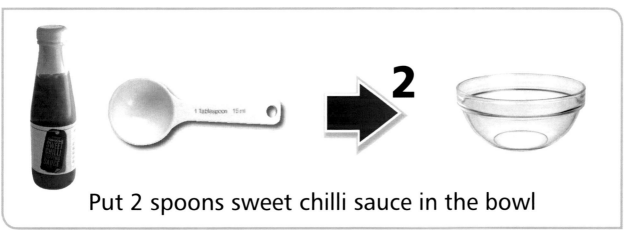

Put 2 spoons sweet chilli sauce in the bowl

Get the **1/4** measuring spoon

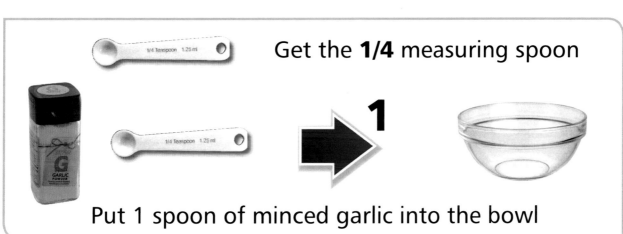

Put 1 spoon of minced garlic into the bowl

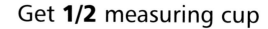
Get **1/2** measuring cup

Fill the cup with peas

Put all the peas into the bowl

 02 00
Set the digital timer for **2 minutes**

Stir everything in the bowl

Keep stirring until the timer makes a noise

When the timer makes a noise

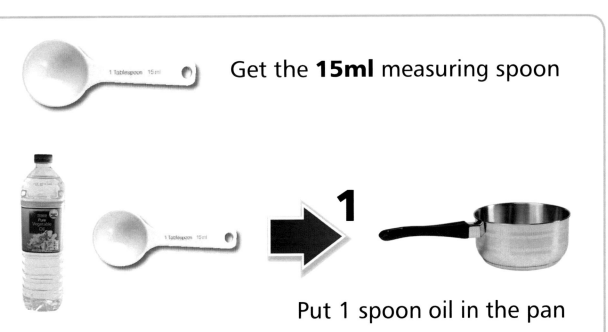

Get the **15ml** measuring spoon

1

Put 1 spoon oil in the pan

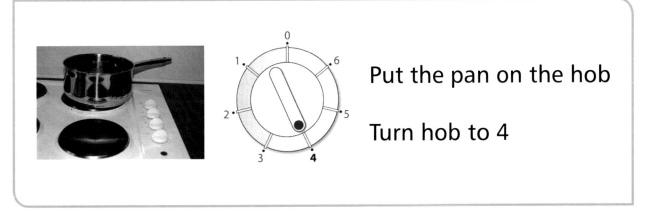

Put the pan on the hob

Turn hob to 4

Put everything from the bowl into the pan

 **06 00** Set the digital timer for **6 minutes**

 Stir everything in the pan

 Keep stirring until the timer makes a noise

 When the timer makes a noise

Put all the noodles in the pan

 **02 00** Set the digital timer for **2 minutes**

Stir everything in the pan

Keep stirring until the timer makes a noise

When the timer makes a noise

 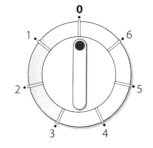

Turn **off** the hob

Put the noodles on a plate

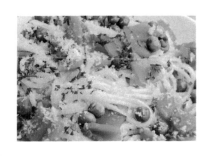

Ready to eat!

Wash up

Put everything away

Prawn and Pea Risotto

 Enough food for 2 meals

 This is a healthy meal
It can help you stay healthy

Food you need

1/2 Measuring cup frozen prawns

1 Vegetable stock cube

5ml Measuring spoon minced garlic

1/2 Measuring cup frozen peas

1 Measuring cup of Arborio rice

1/4 Measuring cup frozen diced onions

15ml Measuring spoon of parmesan cheese

If you can't find something, ask the staff in the shop to help you

Things in the kitchen you need

Digital timer

Electric cooker

Oven gloves

1 Pint measuring jug

Mixing spoon

5ml Measuring spoon

Casserole dish with a lid

Sieve

1 Cup measuring cup

1/4 Measuring cup

Kettle

15ml Measuring spoon

Wash and dry hands

Before you start cooking;

Get out all of the food you need.

Get out all of the things you need to cook with

Turn oven on to 200

 Get the **1** cup measuring cup

Fill the measuring cup with Arborio rice

Put the Arborio rice in the sieve

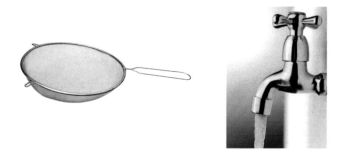

Wash the rice under the tap

Put the rice in the oven dish

Get the **1** cup measuring cup

Put 1 cup of prawns in the oven dish

Get the **1** cup measuring cup

Put 1 cup of peas in the oven dish

 Get the **1/4** measuring cup

Put 1 cup of onions in the oven dish

Put 1 vegetable stock cube in the oven dish

 Get the **5ml** measuring spoon

Put 1 spoon of minced garlic in the oven dish

Fill the kettle to the top line with water

Turn it on

When the kettle has finished boiling

Pour water into the measuring jug to **1/2** pint line

Pour all the water into the oven dish

 02 00

Set the digital timer for **2 minutes**

Stir everything in the oven dish

Keep stirring until the timer makes a noise

When the timer makes a noise

Put the lid on the oven dish

Put oven gloves on

Put oven dish in the oven

40 00

Set the digital timer for **40 minutes**

Come back when the timer makes a noise

When the timer makes a noise

 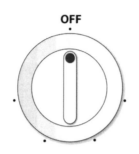 Turn **off** the oven

   Take oven dish out of the oven

Put oven gloves on

 Get the **15ml** measuring spoon

Put 1 spoon parmesan cheese in the oven dish

Ready to eat!

Wash up

Put everything away

Food Safety

Rice can be dangerous

Spores grow in the rice and can make you poorly

It is best to eat it straight away and put any rice in the bin that you don't eat

Tuna and Sweetcorn Pasta Bake

 Enough food for 2 meals

 This is a healthy meal
It can help you stay healthy

Food you need

1 Jar of pasta bake

200g Penne pasta

1 Tin of tuna in spring water

1/2 Measuring cup
grated cheese

1 Measuring cup
frozen sweetcorn

If you can't find something, ask
the staff in the shop to help you

Things in the kitchen you need

Electric cooker

Mixing spoon

Oven gloves

Oven dish

Tin opener

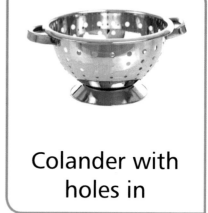

Colander with holes in

1 Pan

Kettle

1 Cup measuring cup

Digital timer

Digital scales

1/2 Measuring cup

Plastic box
with a lid

Wash and dry hands

Before you start cooking;

Get out all of the food you need.

Get out all of the things you need to cook with

 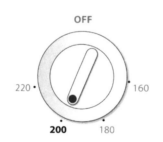

Turn oven on to 200

Weigh 200g of pasta

Put the pasta in the pan

Fill the kettle with water

Turn it on

When the kettle has boiled

Pour water into the pan

Cover the pasta with water

Not to the top of the pan

 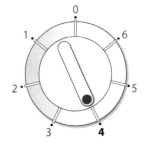

Put the pan on the hob

Turn hob to 4

  Set the digital timer for **10 minutes**

 Stir everything in the pan

Keep stirring until the timer makes a noise

 When the timer makes a noise

OFF

 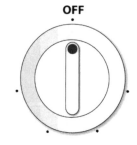 Turn **off** the hob

Take the washing up bowl out of the sink

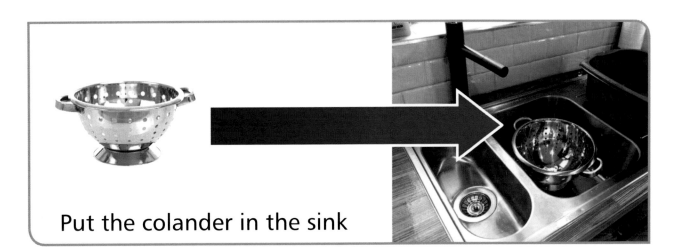

Put the colander in the sink

Pour all the pasta and water into the colander

When all the water has gone

Pour all the pasta into an oven dish

Put all the pasta sauce in the oven dish

Open the tin of tuna

Squeeze the water out of the tuna into the sink

Put tuna in oven dish

Wash and dry hands after touching tuna

Get a **1 cup** measuring cup

Fill the measuring cup with frozen sweetcorn

Put sweetcorn in the oven dish

 02 00 Set the digital timer for **2 minutes**

Stir everything in the oven dish

Keep stirring until the timer makes a noise

 When the timer makes a noise

 Get the **1/2** measuring cup

Fill the cup with cheese

Put the cheese into the oven dish

Put oven gloves on

Put oven dish in the oven

 **25 00**

Set the digital timer for **25 minutes**

Come back when the timer makes a noise

When the timer makes a noise

 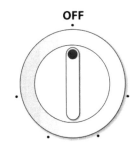 Turn **off** the oven

Put oven gloves on   Take oven dish out of the oven

 Ready to eat!

Wash up

Put everything away

 When the tuna pasta is cold put it in a plastic box with a lid

 Put it in the fridge

 Eat it tomorrow or put in bin

Sausage Casserole

 Enough food for 2 meals

 This is a healthy meal
It can help you stay healthy

Food you need

1 Pack sausage casserole mix

1/3 Measuring cup frozen diced onions

1 Measuring cup frozen mushrooms

1 Tin of beans

1 Tin of potatoes in water (no salt)

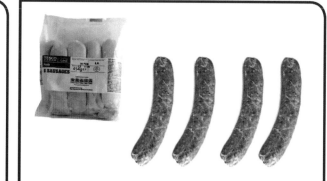

4 Sausages

If you can't find something, ask the staff in the shop to help you

Things in the kitchen you need

Digital timer

Electric cooker

1/3 Measuring cup

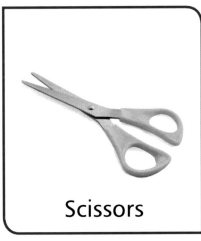

Scissors

Mixing spoon

1 Cup measuring cup

Oven dish

Tin opener

1/2 Measuring cup

Oven gloves

Big pan

Plastic box with a lid

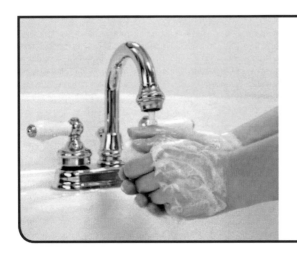

Wash and dry hands

Before you start cooking;

Get out all of the food you need.

Get out all of the things you need to cook with

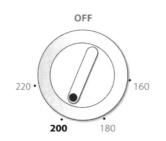

Turn oven on to 200

Get a **1/3** measuring cup

Fill the cup with frozen onions

Pour the frozen onions in the pan

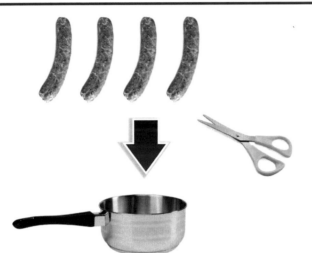

Get 4 sausages

Cut the string on the sausages with scissors

Put 4 sausages in the pan

Wash hands after touching sausages

Get a **1 cup** measuring cup

Fill the cup with frozen mushrooms

Put the mushrooms in the pan

Open the tin of potatoes

Put all the potatoes and water in the pan

Open the tin of beans

Put all the beans in the pan

Get the **1/2** measuring cup

Fill the cup to the top with water

Put all the water in the pan

Open the packet of sausage casserole mix

Put all the mix into the pan

 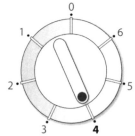

Put the pan on the hob

Turn hob to 4

 **08 00**

Set the digital timer for **8 minutes**

Stir everything in the pan

Keep stirring until the timer makes a noise

When the timer makes a noise

 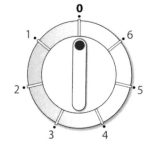

Turn **off** the hob

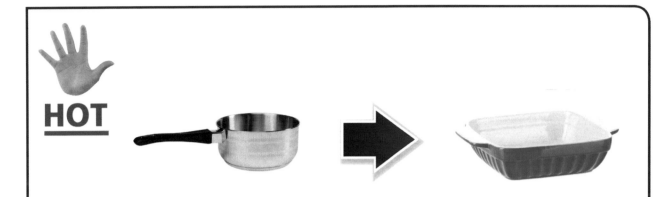

Pour everything from the pan into the oven dish

Put oven gloves on   Put oven dish in the oven

 **60 00** Set the digital timer for **60 minutes**

Come back when the timer makes a noise

When the timer makes a noise

 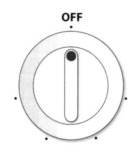

Turn **off** the oven

Put oven gloves on

Take oven dish out of the oven

Ready to eat!

Wash up

Put everything away

When the sausage casserole is cold put it in a plastic box with a lid

Put it in the fridge

Eat it tomorrow or put in bin

Couscous Salad

 Enough food for 2 meals

 This is a healthy meal
It can help you stay healthy

Food you need

1/4 Measuring spoon minced garlic

1/2 Measuring cup couscous

Half cucumber portion

2 Tomatoes

1 Bag of lettuce

1 Tin chickpeas

Vinaigrette dressing

If you can't find something, ask the staff in the shop to help you

Things in the kitchen you need

Digital timer

Kettle

Small bowl

Big mixing bowl

Mixing spoon

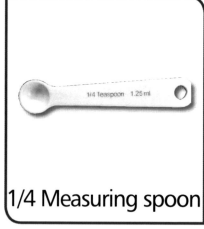

1/4 Measuring spoon

Tin opener

1/2 Measuring cup

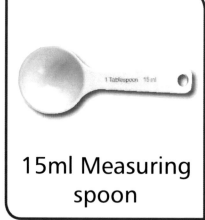

15ml Measuring spoon

Colander with holes in

Chopping knife

Chopping board

Wash and dry hands

Before you start cooking;

Get out all of the food you need.

Get out all of the things you need to cook with

 Get the **1/2** measuring cup

Put 1 cup couscous in the small bowl

 Get the **1/4** measuring spoon

Put 1 spoon of minced garlic in the small bowl

Fill the kettle with water

Turn it on

HOT

When the kettle has finished boiling
Get the **1/2** measuring cup

Put 1 cup of hot water into the small bowl

Put a handful of lettuce in a big mixing bowl

Wash the tomatoes under the tap

Put tomatoes on the chopping board

Chop each tomato into 4 pieces

Put all the tomato in the big mixing bowl

Wash the cucumber under the tap

Put cucumber on chopping board

Chop all the cucumber into pieces

Put all the cucumber in big mixing bowl

Take the washing up bowl out of the sink

Put the colander in the sink

Open the tin of chickpeas

Put all the chickpeas in the colander

Put all the chickpeas into the big mixing bowl

 Get the **15ml** measuring spoon

  **1**

Put 1 spoon vinaigrette dressing in the big mixing bowl

Put everything from small bowl into the big mixing bowl

 02 00 Set the digital timer for **2 minutes**

 Stir everything in the mixing bowl

 Keep stirring until the timer makes a noise

 When the timer makes a noise

 Ready to eat!

 Wash up

Put everything away

Put any salad left in the fridge

Eat it tomorrow or put in bin

Chicken Curry and Naan

 Enough food for 2 meals

 This is a healthy meal
It can help you stay healthy

Food you need

About 400g diced chicken

15ml Measuring spoon vegetable oil

2 Naan bread

1 Jar of curry sauce

If you can't find something, ask the staff in the shop to help you

Things in the kitchen you need

Digital timer

Electric cooker

Tin foil

Plastic box with lid

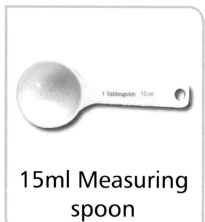

15ml Measuring spoon

Oven gloves

Big pan

Mixing spoon

Oven dish with a lid

Wash and dry hands

Before you start cooking;

Get out all of the food you need.

Get out all of the things you need to cook with

 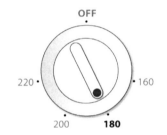

OFF

220 · · 160

200 · **180**

Turn oven on to 180

Wrap 2 Naan in tin foil

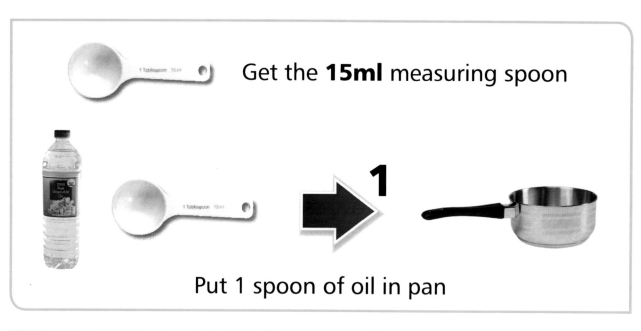

Get the **15ml** measuring spoon

Put 1 spoon of oil in pan

Put all the chicken in the pan

Wash and dry hands after touching the chicken

 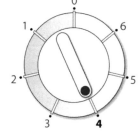

Put the pan on the hob

Turn hob to 4

  Set the digital timer for **6 minutes**

 Stir everything in the pan

Keep stirring until the timer makes a noise

 When the timer makes a noise

 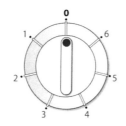 Turn **off** the hob

Put all the chicken in the oven dish

Put all the curry sauce into the oven dish

Put the lid on the oven dish

Put oven gloves on   Put oven dish in the oven

Set the digital timer for **30 minutes**

Come back when the timer makes a noise

When the timer makes a noise

Put the oven gloves on and put the Naan in the oven

Leave the oven dish in the oven

 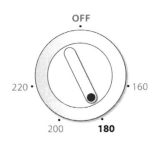 Check the oven is still on at 180

 **0800** Set the digital timer for **8 minutes**

Come back when the timer makes a noise

When the timer makes a noise

 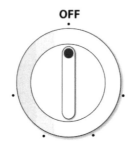
Turn **off** the oven

Put oven gloves on
Take the Naan out of the oven
Take the oven dish out of the oven

HOT

The Naan is **Hot**

Carefully take the
Naan out of the foil

Ready to eat!

Wash up

Put everything away

When the curry is cold put it in a plastic box with a lid

Put it in the fridge

Eat it tomorrow or put in the bin

Mackerel with Roasted Vegetables and Jacket Potato

 Enough food for 1 meal

 This is a healthy meal
It can help you stay healthy

Food you need

1 Ready to eat mackerel fillet

Vegetable oil

1 Pack of roasting vegetables

1 Baking potato

If you can't find something, ask the staff in the shop to help you

Things in the kitchen you need

Digital timer

Electric cooker

Baking tray

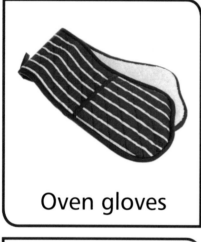
Oven gloves

Dinner plate

Scissors

Fork

Mixing bowl

Fish slice

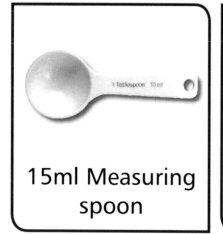
15ml Measuring spoon

Mixing spoon

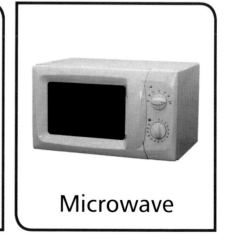
Microwave

 Wash and dry hands

 Before you start cooking;

Get out all of the food you need.

Get out all of the things you need to cook with

 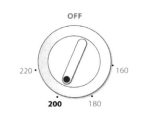 Turn oven on to 200

Put all the roasting vegetables into a mixing bowl

 Get the **15ml** measuring spoon

  **1**

Put 1 spoon vegetable oil in the bowl

  Set the digital timer for **1 minute**

 Stir everything in the bowl

Keep stirring until the timer makes a noise

 When the timer makes a noise

Put everything in the bowl onto the baking tray

 Stab the potato **6** times with a fork

 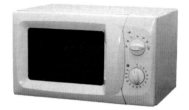

Put potato in microwave, full power for **5 minutes**

When the microwave finishes

Put oven
gloves on

Take potato out
of the microwave

Put oven gloves on

Put the potato in the oven

Put oven
gloves on

Put the baking
tray in the oven

18 00

Set the digital timer for
18 minutes

Come back when the timer makes a noise

When the timer makes a noise

 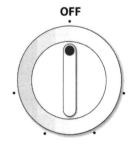

Turn **off** the oven

Put oven
gloves on

Take the baking tray
out of the oven

Put oven gloves on

Take the potato out of the oven

Put the potato on a plate

HOT

Put the roasted vegetables on the plate

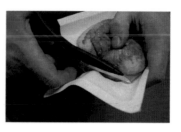

Open the mackerel packet

Get 1 mackerel out

Break the mackerel into pieces with your fingers

Put it on the plate

Wash and dry hands after touching the mackerel

Ready to eat!

Wash up

Put everything away